Christians

Patti -

Hope you enjoy this.

blessings

Donald

**DONALD
SCHMIDT**

**A FIVE SESSION
STUDY GUIDE**

Easter

FOR
Progressive
Christians

WOOD LAKE

Editor: Michael Schwartzentruber
Proofreader: Dianne Greenslade
Designer: Robert MacDonald

Library and Archives Canada Cataloguing in Publication
Title: Easter for progressive Christians.
Names: Schmidt, Donald, 1959- author.
Description: Written by Donald Schmidt. | "Bible study."
| Includes bibliographical references.
Identifiers: Canadiana (print) 20190235640 | Canadiana (ebook) 20190235659
| ISBN 9781773432816
(softcover) | ISBN 9781773432823 (HTML)
Subjects: LCSH: Jesus Christ – Resurrection. | LCSH: Jesus Christ – Appearances.
| LCSH: Easter. | LCSH: Bible. Gospels – Criticism, interpretation, etc.
Classification: LCC BT482 .S36 2020 | DDC 232.9/7–dc23.

Unless otherwise noted, all scripture quotations are taken from the *Common
English Bible*, copyright © 2011, Abingdon, Nashville, TN. Used by permission.
Scripture quotations from *The Message* copyright © by Eugene H. Peterson 1993,
1994, 1995, 1996, 2000, 2001, 2002. Used by permission of NavPress Publishing
Group. The poem "Mary Magdalene's Legacy" first appeared in *Bible Wonderings:
Familiar Tales Retold* by Donald Schmidt copyright © 2006.

ISBN 978-1-77343-281-6

Published by Wood Lake Publishing Inc.
485 Beaver Lake Road, Kelowna, BC Canada V4V 1S5
www.woodlake.com | 250.766.2778

Wood Lake Publishing acknowledges the financial support of the Government of
Canada. Wood Lake also acknowledges the financial support of the Province of
British Columbia through the Book Publishing Tax Credit.

Wood Lake Publishing acknowledges that we operate in the unceded territory of
the Syilx/Okanagan People, and we work to support reconciliation and challenge
the legacies of colonialism. The Syilx/Okanagan territory is a diverse and
beautiful landscape of deserts and lakes, alpine forests and endangered
grasslands. We honour the ancestral stewardship of the Syilx/Okanagan People.

Printed in Canada. Printing 10 9 8 7 6 5 4 3 2 1

CONTENTS

Dedication

To my children and grandchildren who, like the Easter story, remind me in countless ways that tomorrow will always be brighter, and that God is always with us.

Thanks

Sincere gratitude goes to everyone at Wood Lake Publishing, who have an amazing desire to serve the progressive church, especially to Mike Schwartzentruber, editor extraordinaire, who helps an author see through their biases with humour, gentleness, and grace; to Robert MacDonald who designed the book and has made it user-friendly.

For group study

Few stories in the entire pantheon of literature evoke as much emotion as the stories of the resurrection. For many Christians, these are the quintessential stories, the ones that define Christianity, their personal faith, and the whole of human existence. That's a lot of weight to put into a few simple stories!

When using this study in a group setting, it will be helpful to have a sense of where the members of the group are coming from. Are they a mixed group with ideas that are all over the theological map? Do they tend to approach the stories as metaphorical and take the stance that the resurrection could not possibly have happened? Do they take it literally and believe that things must have happened exactly as they are recorded? Do they feel that there is some point to reading these stories, even though they leave us with more questions than answers? Having a sense of this can help you keep the group from getting sidetracked.

It is important for group participants to respect each other. People's ideas may differ – slightly or greatly – and that's absolutely okay. The point of doing this study is not so that everyone comes out with the same belief, nor is it to convince anyone, at any time, that they must believe one thing or another. The purpose of this study is to explore these powerful faith stories so that they might in turn inform and enhance our daily living.

A good facilitator does *not* need to be a biblical scholar of any sort, just someone who can keep the session moving and the conversation on track. Leadership of the group could be held by one person or could change each time, but it is helpful to have a person in charge of the conversation so that the group does not get sidetracked or bogged down.

Spend time with the questions you'll find in the boxes scattered throughout the text; they are designed to provoke reflection. If your group is large – perhaps more than eight to ten people – you might want to divide into smaller groups in order to give people more time to share as they discuss the questions. But remember, whether you discuss the questions in the larger group or in smaller groups, there are no right or wrong answers. The goal is for group members to exchange thoughts, feelings, and opinions. The aim of this guide is not to denigrate the stories we already have, but rather to enhance our understanding of them, and the exchange of ideas is key to achieving this outcome. It's okay for people to disagree. The facilitator should try to hold people's differences of opinion carefully, and help participants respect each other's views.

The facilitator will want to review each session ahead of time to get a sense of how much time to allot to the various questions and themes. The amount of time needed will depend on several factors, such as how many people are in the group, their familiarity with scripture, their theological stance, and so on.

For individual study

The best thing is simply to read the study along with a good translation of the Bible (preferably more than one so you can compare translations). Mark the study guide with interesting things you learn from other sources, or with questions. Spend time pondering the questions that are provided. You might wish to write responses in the margins, but it's far more important to simply let the questions guide your thinking and reflection.

For groups and individuals

If you are not familiar with the concept of myth with regard to biblical stories such as this, you may wish to read and discuss Appendix 3: Myth, Truth, and Fact.

INTRODUCTION

Throughout this study, it may sound at times as though I am trying to prove or disprove the biblical stories, but that is never my intention. If we can be sure of anything, it's that we cannot know for certain what happened. Beyond that, my assumption is always that we should take the biblical stories as they are, we should let them speak for themselves, without injecting into them centuries of tradition.

> For the sake of convenience, throughout this study the authors of the various gospel accounts will simply be referred to by the traditional names of the individuals who are associated with them – Matthew, Mark, Luke, and John – understanding that we do not know the identity of any of them, nor do we even assume that each author wrote their entire gospel.

So what really happened that first Easter Sunday? The simple answer is that no one knows. What we do know, with a fair degree of certainty, is simply this: Jesus was crucified on a Friday, and on Sunday a number of people claimed various encounters with him in a new form. These encounters vary substantially, to the point where there is virtually no consistency. However, that's only a problem if one is trying to prove that each of the stories is factually accurate.

If we suspend that attempt for a moment and read the Easter stories in the gospels for what they are – profound statements of faith – we may discover something powerful and lasting. According to the gospel accounts, several people were convinced that Jesus was somehow present with them from that morning onwards, and their conviction was not going to change. While on Friday they had felt there was no hope, something on that Sunday morning changed their minds. From that point on, a growing number of people began to claim that the presence of Christ was real, that it brought into the present day the teachings of Jesus, and that it promised to continue the project Jesus had begun of changing the world.

This study does not set out to "prove" that Jesus physically rose on Easter Sunday because no one can do that – no scientific evidence can support that claim. But even if such evidence existed, the claim would miss the point. Instead, this study invites participants to engage with the biblical stories of Christ's resurrection in order to understand what the gospel writers meant to tell us, what they wanted us to take from the stories. Ultimately, how you experience Christ in your own life today is what matters – not what might have happened 2,000 years ago. The gospel writers did not set out to prove a point of history, but to tell a story they believed had changed lives already, and would continue to do so.

The first story to look at comes from Mark's gospel, because many scholars believe it was the first one written, and because it's the shortest gospel and the others have all added various pieces to it. We will then look at Matthew, Luke, and finally John, whose account (not surprisingly, given the overall style of that gospel) differs significantly from those of the others. Although this guide explores the differences in the accounts – which are at times quite substantial – the aim, as stated above, is not to prove or disprove, validate or invalidate any particular story or understanding.

Acknowledging, let alone discussing, differences in the Easter stories can be an incendiary act for many people. Again, the purpose of this guide and of doing this exploratory work together is to make the stories come alive for us. After all, someone wrote them down because the stories had transformed their own life and the lives of many others at the time. Hopefully, reading and exploring these stories can in turn enhance our own lives.

Exploring Resurrection, and Mark

Exploring resurrection

Before we look at any of the biblical accounts of that first Easter Sunday, let's spend a little time exploring the idea or concept of resurrection.

Perhaps the first thing to note is that the Bible doesn't really tell us all that much. This is hardly surprising, because the gospel writers are trying to make sense of a story that, well, doesn't really make sense – at least not to a rational mind. No matter what your faith stance is, people do not normally rise from the dead. For Christians, Jesus stands as the only example, and the biblical "evidence" is quite shaky.

This has led people to a variety of positions that roughly fall somewhere between two extremes:

■ Of course Jesus never rose from the dead; people don't do that. Anyone who says so is crazy; or

■ Jesus rose physically from the dead and appeared to lots of people, and you must believe this or you are going to hell.

Most people fall somewhere between these two extremes, but they may not be sure just where exactly – nor are they always sure that they are "allowed" to be where they think they are. To put that another way, many people struggle to accept the idea that Jesus physically rose from the dead, but are afraid to say so while claiming to be Christian. For centuries, the church held up belief in the physical resurrection as a vital litmus test of faith and

acceptance as a Christian. One *had* to believe, which didn't leave much room for questions or wonderings. Such a stance is, I think, simply wrong.

Let me get personal for a moment. My faith in the risen Christ is based on the feeling I have, deep in my being, that somehow the Divine is present in my life in a way that I can't explain, but that is very real to me. The language I use is language about Jesus, because this presence I feel resonates with the stories about Jesus I have heard and explored since childhood. They work, they make sense, and they explain for me some of things that otherwise seem or feel inexplicable. For me, there is no doubt that somehow Jesus "rose from the dead" and is present in my life today. This does *not* mean or require that I believe in a physical resurrection – although, to be fair, it doesn't require me to doubt it, either. For me, the issue doesn't really have anything to do with what might have happened 2,000 years ago; what *really* matters is the experience I have each day as I seek to go about my life, as I seek to live that life as much as possible in accord with the truth that Jesus taught long ago.

■ What does resurrection mean to you?
■ How comfortable are you with people whose views differ – slightly or greatly – from yours on this issue?
■ Is it vital that people share the same opinion as you?
■ How does your faith embrace or exclude these differences?

Perhaps the key thing to remember is that this is a *faith story*; to quote Douglas R. A. Hare, it is not a story "meant to be brought to the jury." Rather, it is a story to help us believe something quite unbelievable. As we shall see, there are a variety of stories of people encountering the risen Christ, including some that are designed to assure us that we really *don't* have to see anything to know or believe.

Mark

Mark 16:1-8

[1]*When the Sabbath was over, Mary Magdalene, Mary the mother of James, and Salome bought spices so that they could go and anoint Jesus' dead body.* [2]*Very early on the first day of the week, just after sunrise, they came to the tomb.* [3]*They were saying to each other, "Who's going to roll the stone away from the entrance for us?"* [4]*When they looked up, they saw that the stone had been rolled away. (And it was a very large stone!)* [5]*Going into the tomb, they saw a young man in a white robe seated on the right side; and they were startled.*

[6]*But he said to them, "Don't be alarmed! You are look-ing for Jesus of Nazareth, who was crucified. He has been raised. He isn't here. Look, here's the place where they laid him.* [7]*Go, tell his disciples, especially Peter, that he is going ahead of you into Galilee. You will see him there, just as he told you."* [8]*Overcome with terror and dread, they fled from the tomb. They said nothing to anyone, because they were afraid.*

This is not a great ending to an awe-inspiring story. In Mark's gospel, some women – the only followers of Jesus to have stayed through everything else – come to the tomb, encounter a stranger, and run away terrified.

That's it.

Editors added additional endings later, to flesh out this rather empty story, but there is not much here. Why? Some scholars think that there was an original ending that got lost, while others think the ending at verse 8 is exactly what Mark intended, because there was no need to share stories of people encountering the risen Christ –

they were everywhere, and well-known. For now, let us simply look at these first eight verses and learn what they can tell us.

Mark 16:1–3 A group of women head to the tomb of Jesus to anoint his body with spices. This is intriguing. Clearly, they expected the body to be there and thus they did *not* expect Jesus to have returned in any form. Indeed, they ask themselves, *"Who's going to roll the stone away...?"* The women have good reason for waiting until Sunday morning, because Jesus died just before Sabbath began. (The Sabbath started on Friday night and continued until Saturday night.) It would have been dangerous, if not pointless, to come after dark on Saturday.

When [the young man in the tomb] said Jesus was not to be found there ... the event we call the resurrection was born.
– Bruce Chilton,
Rabbi Jesus

Mark 16:4 "It was a very large stone." This odd parenthetical comment serves no purpose, but that's what makes it interesting. The women's question in verse 3 implies that the stone is large, so it is intriguing that Mark adds this detail. Perhaps it is to help give some authenticity to the story.

Mark 16:5 Who is the strange, unnamed, young man sitting in the tomb? Some believe it is the mysterious man of Mark 14:51–52, the man in the linen cloth, but this is merely speculation. It is curious that the man in the tomb is not described as an angel. Biblical angels were men who did not look any different from others. Thus the man in the tomb could have been an angel, and it's possible Mark called him a man simply to show that the women did not understand who he was.

Mark 16:6–7 "go tell his [other, male] disciples, especially Peter, that he has been raised, and is going ahead of you into Galilee." This seemingly simple statement holds a profound truth, for the story had "ended" on Friday with the disciples deserting Jesus, and Peter denying him. Now, the risen Christ will meet them in Galilee.

■ What do you make of the young man's statement?
■ How might you hear it, if you were one of the women?

Mark 16:7 Galilee is the hometown of the first disciples, and the place where the ministry to the Gentiles takes place. Thus, the fact that Jesus will meet them there is significant; Jesus will meet them where they live, or lived. Since Galilee is where Jesus' first ministry to the Gentiles took place, it may also mean by implication that *their* ministry is to go beyond Judaism and include the whole world.

Including the Gentiles
Both Mark and Matthew include pieces at the end of their stories about the inclusion of all the world. Over time, Christians came to believe that this ministry is a necessity – that, as Christians, we are called or even required to make sure everyone becomes Christian. Theoretically, this has been the motivation behind most Christian missionary efforts; efforts that involved the colonization of many nations of the world (and often the abuse and mistreatment of their peoples). Other interpreters understand these stories more as invitations; we must open our arms and our hearts to welcome (should they wish to come in) all people, regardless of who they are or where they come from.
■ How do you understand the reference to Galilee? Do you think it's a reference to inclusion, or do you think the disciples are simply being told to "go home," that Jesus will meet them "at home"?
■ How do you understand the difference between a "requirement" and an "invitation" to "include the world"?
■ What are some signs of colonial abuse due to Christian missionary zeal in your part of the world?

Mark 16:8 Biblical literalists must surely stumble over this verse because it is patently false: the women *must* have said something at some point, or no one would know!

> Before proceeding to the alternative endings that were added to Mark over the years, reflect on those first 8 verses.
> ■ If you had never heard anything about the resurrection before, and this was the only story you read (just now, for the first time), what would you make of it?

The other endings of Mark

We have the *King James Version* to thank for what happens next in Mark, or at least in modern English understandings of the story. Interestingly, the *New King James Version* (published in 1982) tries to offer some correction by noting that verses 9–20 are not found in what are considered some of the most accurate Greek manuscripts of the New Testament. However, this is only mentioned in a footnote; the 1982 version still includes the verses. To add to the *King James* problem, the *21st Century King James Version* (published in 1994) leaves out the footnote and includes verses 9–20 as if they are simply part of the text.

This causes difficulties today because Bible translations vary now depending on the market they're aimed at. Translations that cater to the more conservative church tend to include verses 9–20. Some of these translations note that verses 9–20 are not present in all manuscripts, but treat them as if they belong. Translations that tend to cater to more mainline or progressive churches clearly mark them as an obvious addition to the original text.

The editors of the Greek text used by most modern translators emphatically believed that verses 9–20 were added, and pointed out that they are lacking in the "earlier and better" manuscripts. Beyond that, early Christian writers (both Jerome and Eusebius) declared as early as the fourth century that these extra verses were not original. For our purposes, we must understand that Mark either had another ending that has been lost, or that it was intentionally meant to end with verse 8. Verses 9–20 are interesting, but they do not stand on the same footing as the rest of Mark.

Yet someone added them. Why? That's the real question. What purpose do these unusual verses serve?

What has come to be known as the "shorter ending" merely ties off the loose ends of verse 8. But the so-called "longer ending," verses 9–20, includes parallels to stories in Matthew and Luke, and employs a good deal of rhetoric.

The shorter ending
Mark 16:9

[⁹*They promptly reported all of the young man's instructions to those who were with Peter. Afterward, through the work of his disciples, Jesus sent out, from the east to the west, the sacred and undying message of eternal salvation. Amen.*]

Some ancient manuscripts have this short ending that was undoubtedly added simply to give the original chapter 16 a "cleaner" ending. It is indeed tidy, and it solves the "problem" created in verse 8 where it is reported that the women said nothing. If they said nothing, how could word have spread? Furthermore, verse 9 tells us that the disciples – both men and women – continued to share Jesus' message of eternal salvation.

The longer ending

This ending (verses 9–20) is far more problematic because it includes things that are unique to this gospel.

■ Just reading verses 1–8, or adding this shorter ending, how do you think Mark wants us to understand resurrection – as a physical or spiritual event?
■ How do you understand it?

Yet, obviously, at some point, someone wanted it to be considered part of the original, sacred story.

There are more than 10 words or phrases in this longer ending that do not appear anywhere else in Mark, which strongly attests to the fact that these verses were added later. Why? Perhaps we will never know.

Mark 16:9–20

[[⁹*After Jesus rose up early on the first day of the week, he appeared first to Mary Magdalene, from whom he had cast out seven demons.* ¹⁰*She went and reported to the ones who had been with him, who were mourning and weeping.* ¹¹*But even after they heard the news, they didn't believe that Jesus was alive and that Mary had seen him.*

¹²*After that he appeared in a different form to two of them who were walking along in the countryside.* ¹³*When they returned, they reported it to the others, but they didn't believe them.* ¹⁴*Finally he appeared to the eleven while they were eating. Jesus criticized their unbelief and stubbornness because they didn't believe those who saw him after he was raised up.* ¹⁵*He said to them, "Go into the whole world and proclaim the good news to every creature.* ¹⁶*Whoever believes and is baptized will be saved, but whoever doesn't believe will be condemned.* ¹⁷*These signs will be associated with those who believe: they will throw out demons in my name. They will speak in new languages.* ¹⁸*They will pick up snakes with their hands. If they drink anything poisonous, it will not hurt them. They will place their hands on the sick, and they will get well."*

¹⁹*After the Lord Jesus spoke to them, he was lifted up into heaven and sat down on the right side of God.* ²⁰*But they went out and proclaimed the message everywhere. The Lord worked with them, confirming the word by the signs associated with them.]]*

Mark 16:9–11 Echoing stories in both Luke and John, this piece tells us that Mary Magdalene was the first to encounter the risen Christ (although we are not told where). She went to tell the others, but they did not believe her.

Mark 16:12–13 Again seeming to lift a page from Luke, this tells of "two of them walking along in the country-side," which sounds very much like the story of Jesus appearing on the road to Emmaus. Again, however, the story is not believed.

Mark 16:14 Jesus appears to the 11 men who remain of the original 12 male disciples (remember, Judas has died, at least according to Matthew). He scolds them for not believing the others.

> ■ How do you think these verses understand the resurrection of Jesus?
> ■ Does this feel in keeping with verses 1–8, or is it different?

Mark 16:15–16 The statement to preach the good news everywhere, to every creature becomes a problem, for we are told point blank that those who "believe and are baptized" will be saved, but whoever does not believe will be condemned.

> ■ Why do you think this piece might have been added?

Mark 16:17–18 The author undoubtedly means these two verses to be seen as rhetorical.

Mark 16:19–20 Jesus is taken into heaven. This parallels Luke, who describes Jesus being taken away on Easter Sunday. Curiously, in verse 20 we are told that Jesus

("the Lord") worked with the disciples, implying some kind of mystical presence beyond a mere spiritual one.

We are left to wonder why these verses were added. Perhaps it was to bolster those who were seeking to continue the work of the church, offering the veiled "threat" of what would happen if one claimed not to believe. But what are we being called to believe? That Jesus was risen? That Jesus was the son of God? That we are called to subscribe to the new way that Jesus proclaimed on God's behalf?

None of that is made clear. Beyond that, the rhetoric about snake-handling and drinking poison seems strange. The Jesus portrayed in the gospels did not put his followers to such odd tests of faith, so where is all of this coming from?

Snake handling and drinking poison

Some conservative groups take verses 17 and 18 literally, at least to the point of speaking in tongues. Other groups even include handling snakes and drinking poison (I'm not kidding) as part of their Christian worship. According to Wikipedia, there are currently about 40 snake-handling churches in the southeastern United States, and as recently as 2004 there were four in Canada (all in Alberta and British Columbia). In addition, in some of these churches congregants are encouraged to drink poison to demonstrate the strength of their faith. What would inspire/possess people to participate in such a bizarre ritual as handling venomous snakes or drinking known poisons during worship, especially given the fact that perhaps over 100 deaths have been associated with snake handling alone?

Closing Thoughts

People are more familiar with the other gospel accounts of Easter Sunday morning than they are with Mark. It's a strange story, being so short and simple, containing nothing terrifically profound in the first 8 verses, and with some bizarre stories in the later additions. Yet this simple story has power in it.

In his commentary on Mark, Lamar Williamson, Jr. argues strongly for the sudden ending in verse 8. He concludes, "Mark's ending is no ending; only the reader can bring closure."

■ What do you think?

■ Where do you see yourself in this story?

Matthew

Matthew's gospel builds on Mark's very brief account and is therefore similar to it. However, in Matthew's version we also find a rather amusing bit of gossip about the soldiers and a possible cover-up/conspiracy, as well as the story of Jesus ascending into heaven.

Matthew 28:1–10

¹After the Sabbath, at dawn on the first day of the week, Mary Magdalene and the other Mary came to look at the tomb. ²Look, there was a great earthquake, for an angel from the Lord came down from heaven. Coming to the stone, he rolled it away and sat on it. ³Now his face was like lightning and his clothes as white as snow. ⁴The guards were so terrified of him that they shook with fear and became like dead men. ⁵But the angel said to the women, "Don't be afraid. I know that you are looking for Jesus who was crucified. ⁶He isn't here, because he's been raised from the dead, just as he said. Come, see the place where they laid him. ⁷Now hurry, go and tell his disciples, 'He's been raised from the dead. He's going on ahead of you to Galilee. You will see him there.' I've given the message to you."

⁸With great fear and excitement, they hurried away from the tomb and ran to tell his disciples. ⁹But Jesus met them and greeted them. They came and grabbed his feet and worshipped him. ¹⁰Then Jesus said to them, "Don't be afraid. Go and tell my brothers that I am going into Galilee. They will see me there."

Matthew's story begins the same way as Mark's version, although there are some important differences. For example, only two women go to the tomb (Mark had three), there is no mention of spices being brought to anoint the body, and the women do not talk amongst themselves about who will roll away the stone. Verse 1 simply tells us that "Mary Magdalene and the other Mary" went to the tomb.

Matthew 28:1 Who is "the other Mary"? There is another Mary present at the crucifixion, according to Matthew, and presumably she would be the one mentioned here. In 27:56, she is referred to as "the mother of James and Joseph," who were commonly thought to have been Jesus' brothers. The problem is that those were fairly common names, and so is the name Mary (Miriam in Hebrew), so it is hard to tell with any certainty. However, it is not impossible that Mary, the mother of Jesus, discovers the empty tomb.

> ■ If "the other Mary" in verse 1 refers to the mother of Jesus, why might Matthew want to include her?

Matthew 28:2 Matthew's story is unique on this point. Instead of finding the stone rolled away, Matthew inserts this reference to an earthquake. Here it works as a reminder, an echo, of the great star that guided the magi to the infant Jesus; all of creation celebrates the birth of Jesus. At the crucifixion, Matthew tells us that darkness covered the earth from noon until three in the afternoon. And now creation is present, in the form of an earthquake, to proclaim the resurrection.

Matthew 28:4 "became like dead men" Matthew's description of the guards as being like "dead men" is clearly rhetorical; we can assume they fainted. Pause for a moment and imagine the scene: the soldiers, with all their

> **The angel is really God's own presence in mediated form; the earthquake is a drum roll signaling a dramatic act of divine power; and the act of sitting down on the stone is a display of divine strength and authority, as if to say, "Well, so much for that!"**
> **– Thomas G. Long,** *Matthew*

apparent strength, armour, and weaponry, faint while the women do not.

Matthew 28:6 Mark's "he has been raised" is stretched to **"he has been raised from the dead."** This detail may be Matthew's way of clarifying what has happened, that this is a resuscitation of some mysterious kind.

Matthew 28:8 The women flee **"with great fear and excitement,"** which is a bit softer than Mark's "terror and dread." Beyond that, the women run **"to tell the disciples,"** which is substantially different from Mark's "they said nothing to anyone." Clearly Matthew is explaining the obvious – the women *must* have told someone, or the story would have died before it got started.

Matthew 28:9–10 The women encounter Jesus on the road and he greets them. The Greek word used in the text, *chairete*, is often translated as "greetings." Yet the word literally means "rejoice" making this an intriguing first word out of the mouth of the risen Christ. The instruction Jesus gives the women is that they are to go to Galilee and tell the disciples. The choice of Galilee is not a huge surprise, as it was where Jesus had lived out much of his ministry and, perhaps more importantly at this point in the story, it was out of the watchful eyes of the religious leadership and of the Romans.

Matthew 28:10 Luke speaks of apostles, and John of disciples, but Matthew uses the term "brothers" to describe the remaining male disciples. This seems to emphasize how Jesus created a new awareness and understanding of family. (More on this in discussion of the baptismal formula on page 28.)

■ Why do you think Matthew has expanded on Mark's story?
■ How do you understand the differences in the stories?

Matthew 28:11–15

[11]Now as the women were on their way, some of the guards came into the city and told the chief priests everything that had happened. [12]They met with the elders and decided to give a large sum of money to the soldiers. [13]They told them, "Say that Jesus' disciples came at night and stole his body while you were sleeping. [14]And if the governor hears about this, we will take care of it with him so you will have nothing to worry about." [15]So the soldiers took the money and did as they were told. And this report has spread throughout all Judea to this very day.

Let's face it; these guards have a horrible task. In a story that is unique to Matthew, they are charged with guarding the tomb of someone who is dead, to make sure that the body stays there.

In a rush of irony earlier, Matthew had declared that the men charged with guarding the dead became like dead men themselves when confronted with God's proclamation of life. Now, the soldiers go into town, find some of the religious leaders – not their own military leaders, mind you – and tell them what has happened. One has to wonder for a moment what story they actually told, as the details are not very favourable to them: there was an earthquake, some women came, an angel rolled away the stone, they fell to the ground in a dead faint, and the angel declared that they – as well as the religious and Roman authorities – had failed miserably; Jesus had been raised.

The religious authorities respond in a rather predictable way, however. They make up a story about Jesus' body being stolen and bribe the soldiers to spread it, assuring the soldiers that if the governor finds out, they will placate him so that the soldiers don't get into trouble.

Here's the real question, though. If the resurrection is about far more than a physical rising, how do you guard an idea? How do you guard the actions of God? How do you prevent the bold statement that God has brought the presence of Christ into the present tense when the authorities sought to confine it to history? The powers that be had tried to crush what they thought was a small insect but instead unleashed the power of God.

Many scholars think that this addition to the story is Matthew's way of addressing a falsehood circulating in his own time – that some of Jesus' followers snuck to the tomb in the middle of the night, rolled the stone away, and stole the body so that they could then say that the tomb was empty.

> ■ The religious leadership focuses on the lack of a physical body as the critical part of the story, a view that has been shared by many Christians over the centuries. How important is this aspect of the story for you?
> ■ Do you think that the lack of a body in the tomb is key, or is there something else going on? If so, what else might that be?

Matthew 28:16–20

[16]*Now the eleven disciples went to Galilee, to the mountain where Jesus told them to go.* [17]*When they saw him, they worshipped him, but some doubted.* [18]*Jesus came near and spoke to them, "I've received all authority in heaven and on earth.* [19]*Therefore, go and make disciples of all nations, baptizing them in the name of the Father and of the Son and of the Holy Spirit,* [20]*teaching them to*

obey everything that I've commanded you. Look, I myself will be with you every day until the end of this present age."

Matthew 28:17 It is intriguing that, even when they actually see Jesus, some of the 11 disciples still doubt. While much is made of Thomas' doubt in John's gospel, this verse is often ignored. Yet some commentators note the power implicit in this reference, because Jesus makes nothing of it. In other words, it reminds us that doubt does not necessarily conflict with faith.

■ **What do you make of the fact that some of the disciples doubted?**
■ **Do you see doubt as the opposite of faith, or as a necessary component of faith?**

Matthew 28:19 Jesus tells the disciples to **"go and make disciples of all nations,"** a phrase that has caused no end of trouble. The key is how we understand the English given that the Greek is translated fairly literally here. Is Jesus telling us we *must* do this, or that we *can* do this? Certainly those from more conservative traditions tend to read this as a commandment, even as a requirement. For these people, Jesus is saying "you *must* go and make disciples of all people, in all nations" with the implication that something dire could happen – to them, to us, or to both – if we don't do that.

However, there is another way to read this that is far more in keeping with Matthew's church, which is that we *can* do this. In this scenario, Jesus is saying "go and make disciples – not just from my own Jewish community, or from nations that you like, but from all nations." In other words, exclude no one from the possibility of being brought into the family of God's people.

Given that Matthew's gospel was written for a church

that was trying to find ways to move forward as a mixed community of both Jews and Gentiles, this understanding seems to make far more sense.

> ■ **How do you understand Jesus' request/ commandment in verse 19?**
> ■ **How does this influence the way you live your faith?**

Matthew 28:19 "Baptizing them in the name of the Father and of the Son and of the Holy Spirit" Many think that Matthew is inserting into the text the Trinitarian formula that was being used in his church. This possibility seems quite likely. However, we need to use caution. At this point, it is extremely doubtful that this formula had taken on the vast amount of theological and doctrinal baggage it later acquired.

Again, understanding the context of Matthew's gospel and church is most helpful. Matthew is emphasizing "family," and has a very inclusive idea of family at that. This phrase isn't a "cold, mathematical Trinity," to quote Tom Long. Rather, it describes a godly family into which we are all invited. Becoming Christian, for Matthew, is *not* about subscribing to any theological doctrine, but about becoming part of a community that miraculously has room for all manner of people.

The church is to go out to the nations not as an army of occupation but as a humble tutor, teaching mercy and righteousness and forgiveness and peacemaking.
– Thomas G. Long, *Matthew*

Matthew 28:20 "teaching them to obey" Far too many people get excited about the use of the word "obey" here and miss the instruction altogether. To teach people to obey something does not necessarily imply any kind of punishment if they choose *not* to obey. Rather, the emphasis appears to be on the act of *teaching* – of *modelling* with our daily living – ways to be the body of Christ. This is what Matthew was calling his community to, and it is what we are called to do in our modern world. To teach others to obey what Christ taught would be to model justice, compassion, fairness, and equality – all things that by themselves render obsolete the idea of obedience out of fear of punishment.

Closing Thoughts

Matthew's gospel ends with a wonderful phrase, "I myself will be with you every day until the end of this present age." Jesus reminds a community that had experienced the horrors of Good Friday that they will never be alone. In other words, they – and we, by extension – can dare to face any and all injustice, oppression, anger, and hatred knowing that we are not alone. The risen Christ – however we understand that – will be with us.

■ How does Jesus' final statement in Matthew's gospel sit with you?

■ Are there times when this has comforted and/or strengthened you?

■ What might it empower you to do?

Luke

Luke differs substantially from both Matthew and Mark in its telling of what happened on that fateful Sunday. Everything that occurs in this gospel takes place in the one day, in a variety of places. Clearly, the appearances of Jesus to various disciples happened in some mysterious way that cannot be readily explained. It can be argued that the key point Luke wants us to take from his gospel is that the risen Christ is a force, an awareness, a reality that accompanies us on our daily journeys, wherever those journeys may take us.

Luke 24:1–12

1Very early in the morning on the first day of the week, the women went to the tomb, bringing the fragrant spices they had prepared. 2They found the stone rolled away from the tomb, 3but when they went in, they didn't find the body of the Lord Jesus. 4They didn't know what to make of this. Suddenly, two men were standing beside them in gleaming bright clothing. 5The women were frightened and bowed their faces toward the ground, but the men said to them, "Why do you look for the living among the dead? 6He isn't here, but has been raised. Remember what he told you while he was still in Galilee, 7that the Human One must be handed over to sinners, be crucified, and on the third day rise again." 8Then they remembered his words. 9When they returned from the tomb, they reported all these things to the eleven and all the others. 10It was Mary Magdalene, Joanna, Mary the mother of James, and the other women with them who told these things to the apostles. 11Their words struck the

apostles as nonsense, and they didn't believe the women.
[12]But Peter ran to the tomb. When he bent over to look
inside, he saw only the linen cloth. Then he returned
home, wondering what had happened.

A group of women (we do not learn their identities until
verse 10) goes to the tomb early in the morning, where
they find the stone rolled away and nothing inside. They
are greeted by two men in bright clothing who gently
ask, "Why do you look for the living among the dead?"
The men explain what has happened, why the women
shouldn't be surprised that Jesus is not there. Then the
women rush off to tell everyone, only to be laughed at
and scorned by the apostles, except for Peter, who runs
to the tomb, finds it empty, and goes home puzzling over
it all.

Note that there is no encounter with Jesus, no "evidence" in this account except the missing body. The
women tell the others what they encountered but do *not*
proclaim that Jesus is risen, only that they were told that
this had happened.

Luke 24:4–5 The two men appear suddenly, wearing
brilliant clothing – suggesting that they are angelic, that
they are some kind of mysterious, non-human beings. This
may be what Luke wants us to take from the story; however, another school of thought suggests that the "sudden" appearance of beings is a way of saying they may
not have been physically present, but only that their message was *experienced*. This turns the event into a kind of
"aha" moment, as if something were dawning on the
group of women all at once. Of course, we'll never know
which idea Luke intended.

Luke 24:6–8 This piece is crucial. Not only do the
women take the lead (as they do in all four gospel ac-

counts of Easter Sunday) but something else happens as well. The men assume that Jesus had told the women beforehand that he would be betrayed, crucified, and resurrected. This information would normally have only been shared with Jesus' closest friends; thus this simple statement places the women within that inner circle. Undoubtedly this is Luke's way of enlarging the circle, something he will continue to do throughout the book of Acts (which he also wrote), where we see him expanding notions of who is in the church to include Gentiles, leaders who had persecuted the church, those who are excluded for sexual reasons (think of the Ethiopian official in Acts 8) and others.

■ What does it mean to you that the first people to receive the news of the resurrection that first Easter morning were women?
■ In light of our increasing awareness of how the role of women has been suppressed throughout Christian history, what is it like to read accounts such as this, which give a strong nod of support to the presence of women in the early Christian community?

Luke 24:10–11 The translation *The Voice* offers an alternative rendering of these two verses, using verse 10 as a complement to 11, as if to boost the women's credibility: "The Lord's emissaries heard their stories as fiction, a lie; they didn't believe a word of it. (By the way, this group of women included Mary Magdalene, Joanna, and Mary the mother of James, along with a number of others.)"

Luke 24:11 The *King James Version* spoke of how the male disciples heard the testimony of the women as "idle tales" (changed slightly to "an idle tale" in the *New Revised Standard Version* of 1989). Other translations tend to use a term such as "nonsense." Some see a link here between the Greek word *leros* and larynx (throat), which was generally used in Greek to denote depravity; in other words, it's as if the men said to the women "you're nuts."

Luke 24:12 Luke adds this intriguing note about Peter going to the tomb to see what all the fuss is about. Seeing nothing there but a linen cloth, he goes home "wondering what had happened."

■ Had you been Peter in this moment, what thoughts might have been going through your mind?

Luke 24:13–35

¹³On that same day, two disciples were traveling to a village called Emmaus, about seven miles from Jerusalem. ¹⁴They were talking to each other about everything that had happened. ¹⁵While they were discussing these things, Jesus himself arrived and joined them on their journey. ¹⁶They were prevented from recognizing him.

¹⁷He said to them, "What are you talking about as you walk along?" They stopped, their faces downcast.

¹⁸The one named Cleopas replied, "Are you the only visitor to Jerusalem who is unaware of the things that have taken place there over the last few days?"

¹⁹He said to them, "What things?"

They said to him, "The things about Jesus of Nazareth. Because of his powerful deeds and words, he was recognized by God and all the people as a prophet. ²⁰But our chief priests and our leaders handed him over to be sentenced to death, and they crucified him. ²¹We had hoped he was the one who would redeem Israel. All these things happened three days ago. ²²But there's more: Some women from our group have left us stunned. They went to the tomb early this morning ²³and didn't find his body. They came to us saying that they had even seen a vision *of angels who told them he is alive. ²⁴Some of those who were with us went to the tomb and found things just as the women said. They didn't see him."*

²⁵Then Jesus said to them, "You foolish people! Your dull minds keep you from believing all that the prophets talked about. ²⁶Wasn't it necessary for the Christ to suffer these things and then enter into his glory?" ²⁷Then he interpreted for them the things written about himself in all the scriptures, starting with Moses and going through all the Prophets.

²⁸When they came to Emmaus, he acted as if he was going on ahead. ²⁹But they urged him, saying, "Stay with us. It's nearly evening, and the day is almost over." So he went in to stay with them. ³⁰After he took his seat at the table with them, he took the bread, blessed and broke it, and gave it to them. ³¹Their eyes were opened and they recognized him, but he disappeared from their sight. ³²They said to each other, "Weren't our hearts on fire when he spoke to us along the road and when he explained the scriptures for us?"

³³They got up right then and returned to Jerusalem. They found the eleven and their companions gathered together. ³⁴They were saying to each other, "The Lord really has risen! He appeared to Simon!" ³⁵Then the two disciples described what had happened along the road and how Jesus was made known to them as he broke the bread.

The power – and uniqueness – in Luke's Easter account is found in this story of the walk to Emmaus. Two disciples walking down the road have a mysterious encounter with someone, and it leaves them with an overwhelming sense that Christ is risen or, alternatively, that Christ is present with them.

Luke 24:13 "Emmaus, about seven miles from Jerusalem" This would be straightforward except for the fact that there is no place called Emmaus seven miles from Jerusalem. In the Greek text, the distance is given as "60 stadia," which can be measured in a variety of ways. No matter how it's measured, though, the town would be too far for the disciples to walk to it in one afternoon from Jerusalem, and then run back to Jerusalem afterwards. Complicating matters further, some early manuscripts present the name of the place as *Oulammaus*, which was a common Greek transliteration for the mythical place where Jacob was visited by God in a dream. This would be a clue that Luke wants us to know that this is a story, not a factual account.

So are we meant to take this story literally, as proof of the physical presence of Christ (as some scholars have suggested), or as a metaphor or myth meant to show that the resurrection of Jesus occurs within us, when we experience the presence of the living Christ within our hearts?

Luke 24:16 Jesus arrives, but the two disciples do not recognize him. Here the story is similar to John's account of Mary Magdalene encountering the risen Christ in the garden. Interpretations by those who take the story literally run the gamut; some say the disciples didn't recognize Jesus because it was late in the day, or because he had covered his face to shield it from dust, or because he was the last person they expected to see alive. Others, though, who don't view the story as history, understand that Jesus is not physically present – that the "discovery" of Jesus present with them happens through their own conversation.

Luke 24:18 One of the disciples is named Cleopas; the other remains unnamed. This has led many to assume that

New Testament scholars Marcus Borg and John Dominic Crossan suggest that Emmaus is nowhere. Emmaus is nowhere precisely because Emmaus is everywhere. – Rev. Dawn Hutchings, pastor of Holy Cross Lutheran Church, Newmarket, Ontario the second disciple is a woman – perhaps the "wife of Clopas" (a variant spelling of Cleopas), who is mentioned in John's gospel as being one of the women at the foot of the cross. This may be true. Or the presence of a man and a woman (regardless of identity) may be Luke's way of saying "this was an average couple, a man and a woman, on the road to 'anywhere,' and this is what happened to them." It is not an uncommon storytelling technique.

Luke 24:19–24 The two disciples recount for the stranger what has just happened in Jerusalem, interpreting things from what they observed: Jesus was a great teacher, a prophet, but the religious leaders turned him over to the authorities, who killed him. Some women from the group claimed they had found his tomb empty and gave some cock-and-bull story about angels.

Yet this is not the real story, as they are about to learn.

Luke 24:25 Jesus' statement is on par with us saying today, "You just don't get it, do you?" – probably with no small amount of exasperation.

Luke 24:27 The stranger's story about what has occurred begins much earlier and encompasses all that God has done throughout history. This is a seven-mile walk, so there's lots of time to tell all this. And through this telling – whether it is the stranger enlightening the two disciples, or the two disciples discussing it between themselves – they begin to realize that Jesus is *not* gone, but is present with them in that very moment.

Luke 24:30 If this were a factual story, one might expect the stranger to reveal himself earlier. However, there is no spoken revelation, only an action. The stranger sits at table with the disciples, takes bread, blesses it, and breaks it. This is the formula used in the early church –

and still today – for the sacrament of Communion. Jesus, in instituting that action, told the disciples that whenever they did this they were to remember him. Suddenly, the disciples recognize who the stranger is, and immediately the stranger disappears.

Luke 24:34 The two disciples quickly return to Jerusalem – no small feat if they have already walked some seven miles in the hot afternoon sun. Before they can announce their experience, however, they are greeted with the news that Jesus really is risen and has appeared to Simon. (This news comes from the men who just hours before had refused to believe the women!) Jesus, if he is physically risen, seems to be cropping up in multiple places at one time – again, a strong suggestion that we are not meant to take these stories literally.

■ Does it matter to you whether the Emmaus story is factual or made up?
■ How does this story (regardless of factuality) enhance your faith journey?
■ Do we need this story?

Luke 24:36–43

[36]*While they were saying these things, Jesus himself stood among them and said, "Peace be with you!"* [37]*They were terrified and afraid. They thought they were seeing a ghost.*

[38]*He said to them, "Why are you startled? Why are doubts arising in your hearts?* [39]*Look at my hands and my feet. It's really me! Touch me and see, for a ghost doesn't have flesh and bones like you see I have."* [40]*As he said this, he showed them his hands and feet.* [41]*Because they were wondering and questioning in the midst of their happiness, he said to them, "Do you have anything to eat?"* [42]*They gave him a piece of baked fish.* [43]*Taking it, he ate it in front of them.*

[The Emmaus narrative concerns] the evolution of the awareness of the two disciples, from despair over Christ's death to faith in his resurrection.
– Alfred McBride, *The Human Face of Jesus: Luke*

Luke 24:36 Jesus suddenly appears, as if by magic.

Luke 24:38–43 This is an odd passage, which some people believe provides proof that Jesus physically rose from the dead. In the story, Jesus himself challenges the disciples' fear that he is not "real" by daring them to check out his wounds. Then, for good measure, he eats a piece of fish in front of them.

But a story can be true, even if we don't take it literally, even if it's not historical "fact." Many people struggle with this notion because our 21st-century scientific mindset typically requires strong, hard evidence to prove things. We tend to think that a story or perspective without credible evidence has no validity, or can't be true. But this isn't necessarily the case.

Let me give an overly simplistic example from the world of advertising. Advertisers often make statements that are based on interpretation and emotion, because such things cannot be disproven. Just the other day, I drove past two completely different restaurants not connected to each other in any way, both claiming to have the "best burgers in British Columbia." A mind bent on proving things with facts might question this and assume that one of them (or maybe both) are not telling the truth. How can they both be "best"?

The accolade "best" is highly subjective and open to each person's interpretation. Thus, both statements *could* be completely true in the experience of the persons making them, even though they are not the sort of claim that can be proven from a factual or objective standpoint.

In the same way, Luke can present us with a story that tells us, unequivocally, that Jesus was physically present because *to the disciples in that room, Jesus was* present. They could feel his presence and they knew that he was going to be with them forever. How? It didn't, and doesn't, matter. In that moment, they *knew*, and that's *all* that mattered there and then.

⁴⁴Jesus said to them, "These are my words that I spoke to you while I was still with you – that everything written about me in the Law from Moses, the Prophets, and the Psalms must be fulfilled." ⁴⁵Then he opened their minds to understand the scriptures. ⁴⁶He said to them, "This is what is written: the Christ will suffer and rise from the dead on the third day, ⁴⁷and a change of heart and life for the forgiveness of sins must be preached in his name to all nations, beginning from Jerusalem. ⁴⁸You are witnesses of these things. ⁴⁹Look, I'm sending to you what my Father promised, but you are to stay in the city until you have been furnished with heavenly power."

In a close parallel to what happened on the road to Emmaus earlier in the day, Jesus now opens the minds of the disciples to understand the significance of the scriptures and how they relate to him. The challenge here to the disciples – and thus to us – is to realize that the presence of Christ in our lives does not depend on the facts of his life, because his presence (or rather, the presence of God through him) is greater than the life of one individual.

Luke 24:46 Speaking with the two disciples, Jesus apparently references scriptures that say the Messiah (the Christ) will suffer, die, and be resurrected. The problem is, such a scripture does not currently exist. Perhaps there was a piece of writing, no longer available, that said this. More likely it was a spoken belief – either that Jesus had heard or that Luke had heard – which may have carried the weight of written scripture. Such a thing is not uncommon even in modern culture; today people will especially claim they saw something on the internet, whether they did or didn't, as a way of giving it more credibility.

Luke 24:47 This passage does *not* mean or even imply that everyone must be converted to Christianity, but simply that the invitation to new life and forgiveness must be offered to everyone. Too often we confuse those two.

Luke 24:50–53

50He led them out as far as Bethany, where he lifted his hands and blessed them. 51As he blessed them, he left them and was taken up to heaven. 52They worshipped him and returned to Jerusalem overwhelmed with joy. 53And they were continuously in the temple praising God.

Luke 24:51 Jesus departs on the evening of that first Easter Day. This appears to contradict the story in Acts, where Jesus departs 40 days later. Again, we are invited to do one of three things: 1. argue vociferously over which story is correct, 2. try to reconcile the two, or 3. ask if it really matters which version is correct. Personally, I prefer the third option. The key for Luke seems to be to tell us that Jesus has departed, leaving his ministry in the hands of those who have followed him.

Closing Thoughts

Whether Luke wanted his stories to be read as factual accounts (thus, a physical resurrection) or to be understood as myth – for more on this, see Appendix 3: Myth, Truth, and Fact – is not something we can discern with any certainty. But it's not the real point. Luke has presented stories that transcend the need for fact or proof. Instead, he shows us a variety of ways in which everyone – including those of us in the 21st century – can experience the risen Christ. When we doubt, when we are unsure, when we don't know where we are going or what's going to happen, Jesus comes to us, and is present with us.

■ What does it mean to you that Jesus is risen?
■ How is Christ present in your daily living?
■ How do the stories in Luke's gospel inform that?

John 20

John's gospel provides us with the longest account of the events on Easter Day and following. Having said that, most scholars generally assume that the original gospel ended after chapter 20 and that chapter 21 is an addition. The stories that this gospel tells are distinctly different than those in the synoptic gospels (Matthew, Mark, and Luke), and provide us with a very important – although quite different – message.

It is helpful to keep in mind, especially as we encounter the differences in John's gospel, that John was not concerned with historical facts. Rather, for this author, symbolism was far more important. Thus, in order to make a point, John has no problem changing the order or sequence of the stories from the chronology presented in the other gospels. We'll see this in chapter 21.

John 20:1–10

[1]Early in the morning of the first day of the week, while it was still dark, Mary Magdalene came to the tomb and saw that the stone had been taken away from the tomb. [2]She ran to Simon Peter and the other disciple, the one whom Jesus loved, and said, "They have taken the Lord from the tomb, and we don't know where they've put him." [3]Peter and the other disciple left to go to the tomb. [4]They were running together, but the other disciple ran faster than Peter and was the first to arrive at the tomb. [5]Bending down to take a look, he saw the linen cloths lying there, but he didn't go in. [6]Following him, Simon Peter entered the tomb and saw the linen cloths lying there. [7]He also saw the face cloth that had been on Jesus'

> If you have time, you might wish to explore Appendix 2 – Mary Magdalene: Apostle, not Prostitute as part of your study of John 20. It has been placed in an appendix in order to give it more room.

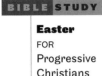
head. It wasn't with the other clothes but was folded up in its own place. ⁸Then the other disciple, the one who arrived at the tomb first, also went inside. He saw and believed. ⁹They didn't yet understand the scripture that Jesus must rise from the dead. ¹⁰Then the disciples returned to the place where they were staying.

John 20:1 As in the other gospels, this story happens early in the morning. However, unlike the others, in this story Mary Magdalene goes to the tomb by herself. As a piece of history, this is doubtful since it was never safe for a woman to travel alone, especially "while it was still dark," but it fits with John's story.

John 20:2 Mary runs to tell Peter what she has seen. However, in this version she merely states the simple fact that the tomb is empty – someone has taken Jesus' body, and she doesn't know where they placed it. This story, while different from the others makes perfect sense.

John 20:8 Peter and "the other disciple" rush to the tomb, and are confused more than anything else. However, when the second disciple (not named but generally understood to be John) enters the tomb, his response to the visual evidence is to believe. Believe what? We are not told. Presumably he at least believed that Jesus' body had been taken. Does he also believe that Jesus is somehow risen? We cannot know, although that is what many take from this story.

John 20:9 John tells us that "they" (Peter and the other disciple and, possibly, Mary) did not yet understand what the scriptures had said that Jesus must rise from the dead. The problem with this verse is twofold: first, we were just told in the previous verse that John "believed," although we do not know what he believed. Second, what scriptures is John referring to? The only "scriptures" at that time were the Hebrew scriptures, what some Christians now refer to as the Old Testament. Nothing in the Hebrew scriptures speak of Jesus, or any other messiah, being crucified and then resurrected.

The easiest way to deal with a verse like this is simply to ignore it – doing so is hardly dishonest, but simply a way of admitting that the author must have had something in mind, though we don't know what.

John 20:11–18

[11]*Mary stood outside near the tomb, crying. As she cried, she bent down to look into the tomb.* [12]*She saw two angels dressed in white, seated where the body of Jesus had been, one at the head and one at the foot.* [13]*The angels asked her, "Woman, why are you crying?"*

She replied, "They have taken away my Lord, and I don't know where they've put him." [14]*As soon as she had said this, she turned around and saw Jesus standing there, but she didn't know it was Jesus.*

[15]*Jesus said to her, "Woman, why are you crying? Who are you looking for?"*

Thinking he was the gardener, she replied, "Sir, if you have carried him away, tell me where you have put him and I will get him."

[16]*Jesus said to her, "Mary."*

She turned and said to him in Aramaic, "Rabbouni" (which means Teacher).

[17]*Jesus said to her, "Don't hold on to me, for I haven't yet gone up to my Father. Go to my brothers and sisters and tell them, 'I'm going up to my Father and your Father, to my God and your God.'"*

[18]*Mary Magdalene left and announced to the disciples, "I've seen the Lord." Then she told them what he said to her.*

This is a powerful story, unique to John's gospel. It tells of a very intimate and personal encounter between Mary and the risen Christ. Most importantly, Jesus seems to commission Mary as the first apostle of the resurrection. Some interpreters even see in verse 17 an example of Jesus ordaining a woman.

John 20:12 Presumably the angels have just now appeared. They ask her why she is crying.

John 20:14 Jesus appears, although as in Luke's story about the disciples on the road to Emmaus, he is not recognized. Mary thinks he is the gardener. Some commentators suggest that this is because she is seeing through tears, it is still very early in the morning and there is not much light, and she does not expect Jesus to be there. All of these explanations are plausible but are only required if we are looking for a factual story.

John 20:16 In this climactic verse, Jesus calls Mary by name. She immediately responds with the Aramaic title that those closest to Jesus would have used, *Rabbouni*, which we are then told means "teacher." Actually, it is a term of both endearment and admiration, more akin to "My dear teacher" – not in any condescending way, but as a term of great respect. The fact that this conversation is presented in Aramaic, the language Mary and Jesus would have spoken, gives it added strength. The truth behind the powerful myth being shared here is that the risen Christ knows each of us and calls us by name. God's intimate love for each of us cannot ever be diminished.

John 20:17 Jesus tells Mary not to touch him, an indication that he is not physically present.

■ Many see in this verse Jesus commissioning Mary as the first apostle of the resurrection. Others see here Jesus ordaining her to a prophetic ministry. How do you understand verse 17?

■ For around 2,000 years, Christianity has generally oppressed women, and the majority of Christians worldwide do not accept the ordination of women. How do you reconcile that with verse 17?

John 20:19–29

19It was still the first day of the week. That evening, while the disciples were behind closed doors because they were afraid of the Jewish authorities, Jesus came and stood among them. He said, "Peace be with you." 20After he said this, he showed them his hands and his side. When the disciples saw the Lord, they were filled with joy. 21Jesus said to them again, "Peace be with you. As the Father sent me, so I am sending you." 22Then he breathed on them and said, "Receive the Holy Spirit. 23If you forgive anyone's sins, they are forgiven; if you don't forgive them, they aren't forgiven."

24Thomas, the one called Didymus, one of the Twelve, wasn't with the disciples when Jesus came. 25The other disciples told him, "We've seen the Lord!"

But he replied, "Unless I see the nail marks in his hands, put my finger in the wounds left by the nails, and put my hand into his side, I won't believe."

26After eight days his disciples were again in a house and Thomas was with them. Even though the doors were locked, Jesus entered and stood among them. He said, "Peace be with you." 27Then he said to Thomas, "Put your finger here. Look at my hands. Put your hand into my side. No more disbelief. Believe!"

28Thomas responded to Jesus, "My Lord and my God!"

Easter
FOR
Progressive
Christians

²⁹Jesus replied, "Do you believe because you see me? Happy are those who don't see and yet believe."

The male disciples are hiding. It is important to digest this piece before continuing on. Mary Magdalene went to the tomb on her own (in this gospel) and then shared the news of resurrection with Peter and the beloved disciple. Peter then goes home, wondering, yet we can assume that at some point later in the day he told the other disciples and they decided to hide out in a locked room.

Many people immediately leap to their defence claiming that they had to hide because it was not safe for them as (male) followers of Jesus, whereas it would have been okay for the women to remain at large. There is nothing to back this up, however, other than a strong desire to redeem the role of the men. We must not ignore that rather than go out and proclaim – or even simply talk about – the good news that Christ is no longer in the tomb but is somehow risen, they chose to hide themselves in a locked room.

Then [Jesus] took a deep breath and breathed into them. "Receive the Holy Spirit," he said. "If you forgive someone's sins, they're gone for good. If you don't forgive sins, what are you going to do with them?"
– John 20:22–23, *The Message*

John 20:19 This is still Easter Day, and the disciples have hidden behind closed doors because they are afraid of the religious authorities. This, however, does not stop Jesus, who miraculously enters the room and simply greets them. The words "Peace be with you" can take on a profound theological bent, but they are simply a standard greeting; some have suggested it's like Jesus suddenly appeared and said, "Hey there."

John 20:22–23 Here Jesus sends his holy spirit upon the gathered disciples, and sends them out to forgive people's sins.

Forgiveness

There is a wide range of interpretation on the instruction to forgive, with the addition that if you forgive someone's sins they are forgiven, and if you do not, they are not forgiven. Some see here a note of judgment – the ones that Jesus (and by later extension the church) ordains/commissions have the power to decide who merits forgiveness. Others see instead that more weight is placed upon the disciples (and thus, arguably, on us): you need to forgive the sins of others, or else they will be forced to carry them around and live in a state of being unforgiven. To refuse to forgive would be nothing less than going against Christ.

■ How do you understand forgiveness?
■ When has being forgiven had a profound effect on you?
■ When has not being forgiven had a profound effect on you?
■ What are situations where it is difficult (or even impossible) to forgive?

John 20:24 "Didymus" simply means "twin." Earlier scholars suggested that the nickname was given to Thomas because of his dual role of believer and doubter, but there is nothing to support this. Rather, the easiest and most plausible explanation is that he looked like one of the other disciples, or Jesus, and thus earned the nickname. As has been the case in many other parts of the overall story, this fact is moot if one is not looking to explain the story literally.

John 20:25 Thomas' statement ought to be understood as rhetoric. Why should he believe their story – it seems ridiculous to think that Jesus (who had been killed a few days before) miraculously appeared in a locked room, and then disappeared again.

John 20:26 "after eight days" This is the Jewish way of saying "a week later." Again, Jesus appears miraculously through a locked door. It is worth noting that rather than going out and proclaiming any good news (or offering forgiveness as Jesus told them to do a week before) the disciples are still hiding out in fear. There is a great irony here – Thomas is referred to as the doubter, and yet the disciples are the ones who are hiding!

John 20:27 Given that Jesus has somehow appeared through a locked door, it is odd that he invites Thomas into a rather physical verification process. Presumably this is rhetorical.

John 20:29 Jesus' comment here is a classic John-style statement and should be seen for its power: it emphasizes that all those who come to faith from that moment on are blessed/happy (it is the same word in Greek). For John, this is an important emphasis and it's where he essentially leaves off his story of Jesus. We who do not see the risen Christ, who have no physical evidence whatsoever, do not need that – the experience of Christ with us (even in locked rooms) is sufficient.

John 20:30–31

30Then Jesus did many other miraculous signs in his disciples' presence, signs that aren't recorded in this scroll. 31But these things are written so that you will believe that Jesus is the Christ, God's Son, and that believing, you will have life in his name.

This short piece strongly implies that the gospel originally ended here, and thus that chapter 21 is an addition. This does not render John 21 any less important, but does suggest that it was added later, and probably comes from a different writer. As we shall see, it contains stories that do not appear (at least not in this form) in the other gospels.

Closing Thoughts

John's gospel is one of the most popular and beloved books in the New Testament. It opens with the great poem that states, "In the beginning was the word, and the word was with God, and the Word *was* God..." It contains astonishing stories such as the wedding at Cana, the healing of the blind man at the pool of Siloam, and the raising of Lazarus, not to mention the profound story of Jesus washing the feet of the disciples rather than running away from imminent danger, modelling the epitome of servant leadership. Finally, it contains the astonishing and powerful story of Mary Magdalene being called by name in the garden – a beautiful reminder that no matter who we are or where we might find ourselves, the risen Christ calls us, knows us, and loves us.

Given all of that, it can be difficult to accept that the book may be primarily a work of "fiction" (to use the modern understanding of that word), certainly more so than the other gospels.

■ How does the possible "mythic" nature of John's gospel sit with you?

■ What do you take from its stories, regardless of whether they are factual or not?

■ What do you think John is trying to tell us?

John 21

Virtually all scholars believe that John 21 is an addition written by someone other than the author of the rest of the gospel, sometime after the deaths of both Peter and the beloved disciple. As if the ending of John 20 were not enough to suggest this, the different style of subject matter of John 21, and the use of some vocabulary that appears nowhere else in the gospel, strongly suggests different authorship.

Does this mean it is not scripture? Of course not. It simply means that it comes from another source. The stories presented here are no less valid than those found elsewhere, and the truths they present are of great value in understanding how Christians are invited to live their lives in the glorious "shadow" of the empty tomb.

John 21:1–14

¹Later, Jesus himself appeared again to his disciples at the Sea of Tiberias. This is how it happened: ²Simon Peter, Thomas (called Didymus), Nathanael from Cana in Galilee, Zebedee's sons, and two other disciples were together. ³Simon Peter told them, "I'm going fishing."

They said, "We'll go with you." They set out in a boat, but throughout the night they caught nothing. ⁴Early in the morning, Jesus stood on the shore, but the disciples didn't realize it was Jesus.

⁵Jesus called to them, "Children, have you caught anything to eat?"

They answered him, "No."

⁶He said, "Cast your net on the right side of the boat and you will find some."

So they did, and there were so many fish that they couldn't haul in the net. ⁷Then the disciple whom Jesus loved said to Peter, "It's the Lord!" When Simon Peter heard it was the Lord, he wrapped his coat around himself (for he was naked) and jumped into the water. ⁸The other disciples followed in the boat, dragging the net full of fish, for they weren't far from shore, only about one hundred yards.

⁹When they landed, they saw a fire there, with fish on it, and some bread. ¹⁰Jesus said to them, "Bring some of the fish that you've just caught." ¹¹Simon Peter got up and pulled the net to shore. It was full of large fish, one hundred fifty-three of them. Yet the net hadn't torn, even with so many fish. ¹²Jesus said to them, "Come and have breakfast." None of the disciples could bring themselves to ask him, "Who are you?" They knew it was the Lord. ¹³Jesus came, took the bread, and gave it to them. He did the same with the fish. ¹⁴This was now the third time Jesus appeared to his disciples after he was raised from the dead.

John places here a story that appears in Luke 5:1–11, although with a unique flavour that only this gospel writer can add. It is possible that John had the story from another source (probably not the actual book of Luke, but another source that Luke might also have used) and saw here the basis for some great symbolism, as we shall see.

John 21:1 Twice we are told that Jesus "showed himself" (or "revealed" himself in some translations). This has always been John's way of telling us that this is a profound and miraculous appearance. Part of the significance, which we also see in John's account of Jesus' masterly control of the entire passion narrative – see *Death of Jesus for Progressive Christians* – is that Jesus is also in complete control of things *after* the resurrection.

John 21:2 Nathanael appears here in the list of disciples. The others have all appeared at various times in the story, but we haven't seen Nathanael since John 1:50. However, at that time, Jesus promised Nathanael that he would see "even greater things" in times to come. Is that what is about to happen now in chapter 21? Is this John's way of telling us that, by staying faithful, Nathanael is now rewarded with what was promised before? It seems too obvious to be coincidence. This becomes, then, a reminder to those who will come later that they ought to stick it out because if they do they, too, will see even greater things.

John 21:4 Again Jesus appears but is not recognized. This has happened several times now and it is a strong indication that the risen Christ is *experienced* rather than physically seen. It is also worth noting that Jesus appears at daybreak – such a powerful symbol. John 20 began with Mary going to the tomb "while it was still dark." Now Jesus shows himself once again in the dawning of a new day.

> ■ How does Jesus bring the light of a new day into your life?
> ■ Just as Jesus' presence in this new light enabled the disciples to complete their work, how does the presence of the risen Christ enhance your daily living?

John 21:5 Jesus' odd name for the disciples ("children") is thought to be a bad Greek rendering of what could have been a common Aramaic expression, probably closer to "guys" or "gentlemen" in our modern use. It is not meant as a term of demotion, but of endearment.

John 21:6 While the disciples have returned to doing what they know, and to doing it in the old familiar way,

Jesus appears to challenge them to live their lives differently, in light of the resurrection. They are called to cast their net on the other side of the boat – in other words, to continue their lives in the manner which Jesus modelled for them – from this point onwards.

John 21:7 As happened at the tomb, where the beloved disciple "believed" and Peter went home puzzled, here it is John (the "beloved disciple") who proclaims who Jesus is. Simon Peter responds by getting dressed – fishermen commonly wore only a simple loincloth – and jumping into the water.

John 21:9–10 What a delightful image – Jesus cooking breakfast for the disciples! This is not unlike Jesus' courageous and bold act of washing their feet the night before he was killed. As we saw there, so we see here Jesus modelling ministry that is about serving others.

John 21:10 Jesus invites the disciples to bring some of the fish they have caught – a symbol that the work of Jesus (cooking breakfast) and of the disciples (catching fish) are connected. We are called to continue doing Jesus' work in the world.

John 21:11 The number 153 is clearly symbolic. It was thought to be the number of nations in the known world at the time John was writing his gospel (remember, nations were much smaller designations). Thus, this is a powerful way of stating that in the church (symbolized by the net) there is room for all kinds of people, from every nation in the world. Amazingly, even though obviously some of these fish would have been "natural enemies" of others in the net, the net is not torn. This is a clear statement about the need for the church to be inclusive, even though it will take some effort at times – as

witnessed by the disciples' difficulty in bringing this massive net to shore.

Another explanation has been found in the suggestion that this was the number of Christians in the early community. While the number may seem quite small, it is not out of the question; Acts 1:15 tells us that the church in the first weeks numbered about 120. If this is what the reference means, then it may be a strong suggestion that there is room for all within one net – implying that we must find ways to get along and to work together.

> ■ **How do you understand the inclusive nature of the church?**
> ■ **Is there truly room for *all* in the church?**
> ■ **If there are limits, how does one determine what they might be?**

John 21:13 Some in the early church understood this feeding of the disciples as a new form of the Last Supper (a story that is absent in John's gospel). It has been suggested that some early Christian communities used bread and fish, rather than bread and wine, as the elements of communion.

The fish

The fish is the earliest Christian symbol. Many have noted that the letters of the Greek alphabet which form the word for fish – *ichthus (ICK-thoos)* – could be abbreviations for "Jesus Christ, God's Son, Saviour." When they were being severely persecuted, Christians may also have used the fish as a secret symbol by which they could identify each other. One person would draw the upper half of a simple fish (a single line similar to a half moon or raised eyebrow) in the dirt; if the other person were not a Christian they would presumably assume this was a doodle. However, if they *were* a Christian they would complete the fish with a corresponding line below. This story, while popular, has been called into question by several scholars. However, we *do* know that the word and image of a fish have been connected with Christ from the first days of Christianity.

15When they finished eating, Jesus asked Simon Peter, "Simon son of John, do you love me more than these?"

Simon replied, "Yes, Lord, you know I love you."

Jesus said to him, "Feed my lambs." 16Jesus asked a second time, "Simon son of John, do you love me?"

Simon replied, "Yes, Lord, you know I love you."

Jesus said to him, "Take care of my sheep." 17He asked a third time, "Simon son of John, do you love me?"

Peter was sad that Jesus asked him a third time, "Do you love me?" He replied, "Lord, you know everything; you know I love you."

Jesus said to him, "Feed my sheep. 18I assure you that when you were younger you tied your own belt and walked around wherever you wanted. When you grow old, you will stretch out your hands and another will tie your belt and lead you where you don't want to go." 19He said this to show the kind of death by which Peter would glorify God. After saying this, Jesus said to Peter, "Follow me."

Here the story shifts to an emphasis on Simon Peter, perhaps to counterbalance the emphasis on Mary Magdalene in the previous chapter (see Appendix 3 – Mary Magdalene: Apostle, not Prostitute, on p. 61).

Jesus asks Peter three times if he loves him and Peter gets rather annoyed at the repetition. It seems logical that the three questions are intended to counterbalance Peter's three denials. These previous denials of Jesus do not exempt Peter from further discipleship, nor do they exempt him from receiving any of the benefits of belonging to the Christian community.

John 21:18–19 When Peter was younger, he could do what he wanted. Now that he has declared his allegiance to Jesus and to the ministry that Jesus began, his days are

■ What does it feel like to be pardoned for something you have done wrong?
■ How does that enable you to have a new beginning?

(symbolically, at least) numbered. Following Jesus can get one killed, just as Jesus was killed. This is part of the resurrection story: to stay committed to God's promise as presented by Jesus is to ensure the anger of those in authority who wish to maintain the status quo at all costs.

John 21:20–23

²⁰Peter turned around and saw the disciple whom Jesus loved following them. This was the one who had leaned against Jesus at the meal and asked him, "Lord, who is going to betray you?" ²¹When Peter saw this disciple, he said to Jesus, "Lord, what about him?"

²²Jesus replied, "If I want him to remain until I come, what difference does that make to you? You must follow me." ²³Therefore, the word spread among the brothers and sisters that this disciple wouldn't die. However, Jesus didn't say he wouldn't die, but only, "If I want him to remain until I come, what difference does that make to you?"

Phileo or agape?

A great deal has been made of the fact that John inserts two different words for love into the questions Jesus asks of Peter. Specifically, Jesus uses *agape* in verses 15 and 16, and then *phileo* in verse 17. Numerous sermons have been preached on the significance of these two words for love and on the apparent "rank" in them. But there are huge problems with doing this.

First, *agape* (a selfless love that knows no boundaries) is generally considered to be of greater value than *phileo* (understood as familiar or "brotherly" love). If this is the case, it seems odd that Jesus would begin his questions with the higher form, and then revert to a lesser one. Would not the opposite order make more sense? Second, the words tend to be used somewhat interchangeably throughout the gospel of John.

This reminds us that the point of the story presented here is not to contrast two Greek words, but rather to emphasize Jesus' concern for Peter's commitment to continuing the ministry that Jesus began.

John 21:21 Peter's question "Lord, what about him?" can also be translated as "What is to become of him?" which seems a little closer to what Peter probably would have asked.

John 21:22 The whole interchange regarding the beloved disciple (verses 20–23) seems inserted to counter some rumour that was current at the time the text was being written. While this is only conjecture, it seems the rumour must have been something about this disciple living forever, or at least staying alive until Jesus returned. A common belief in the early church was that Christ would return before any faithful Christians died. Obviously, that did not happen. Paul addresses this in 1 Thessalonians, and John addresses it here, albeit in a conversation about one individual.

It is also important to note that the verb "to remain" does not necessarily mean "to remain alive" and thus Jesus could simply be saying, "If I want him to remain a part of the Christian community, what does that have to do with you? I want you to follow me; don't concern yourself with others." This could be a way of reminding Christians to focus on their own ministry and not worry about that of others.

John 21:24–25

²⁴*This is the disciple who testifies concerning these things and who wrote them down. We know that his testimony is true.*

²⁵*Jesus did many other things as well. If all of them were recorded, I imagine the world itself wouldn't have enough room for the scrolls that would be written.*

John 21:24 This verse is often seen as trying to imply that the beloved disciple (generally assumed by scholars as being John, son of Zebedee and brother of James) is

BIBLE STUDY

Easter
FOR
Progressive
Christians

I figure, when they're shooting at you it's because you must be doing something right.
– *The West Wing*

the author of this gospel. This may or may not be the implication, but either way it's not based on fact; all of the initial disciples would have been long dead before the gospel of John, let alone chapter 21, was written (somewhere around 90–100 CE).

John 21:25 This unbridled, superlative tidbit is a fitting way to end the gospel and, because of their order in the New Testament, the full span of all four gospels.

Additionally, it is important to note that, unlike Matthew and Luke, there is no ascension story in John. Jesus does not leave. Given that John, perhaps more than the others, strongly suggests a risen Christ who is spiritually present but not physically present, this is significant. The "many other things that Jesus did" continue to this day, in the works of those who seek to be followers of Jesus.

Final Thoughts

Clearly, the four gospel writers wish to make different points about what the resurrection of Jesus meant to them. These meanings carry forward to our lives as modern-day disciples. We can summarize these differences as follows.

Mark does not really tell us much about the resurrection at all and, if we assume that he meant for his book to end at chapter 16, verse 8, he leaves us with a sense of pure wonder. The tomb is empty. What does that mean to you?

Matthew wants us to know that the created world responded to the empty tomb in the same way that it responded to the baby in a manger; and that the church will continue as long as we welcome all nations and remember that Christ is with us forever.

Luke presents a number of stories and in so doing shows the disciples grappling with the new reality presented by the empty tomb. Jesus is the completion of history, of God's saving acts through the *Torah*, the prophets, and the psalms. We – Christ's followers – are called to proclaim to all the world a change of heart and new life as a result of forgiveness.

John offers a rather mystical, spiritual Christ who calls people by name, and who makes a point of pardoning the one who denied knowing him. He sends the disciples out to proclaim forgiveness in his name, and continues – even now – to do all sorts of wonderful things.

■ Which story do you like the best, and why?

■ How does each story inform your understanding of the risen Christ?

Comparison Chart of Resurrection Appearances

	Mark	Matthew	Luke	John
When?	At sunrise on the first day of the week	At dawn on Sunday	Very early Sunday morning	Early Sunday morning, while it was still dark
Who goes to the tomb?	Mary Magdalene, Mary the mother of James, Salome	Mary Magdalene and "the other Mary"	Mary Magdalene, Joanna, Mary the mother of James, the "other women"; then Peter	Mary Magdalene, then Peter and "the other" disciple
Who greets them?	A young man	An angel of the Lord	Two men	No one
Who encounters Christ?	No one	The women, running from the tomb	Two disciples, later in the day, on the road to Emmaus	Mary, in the garden
What happens after?	Women run away, afraid	Soldiers and religious authorities conspire a lie; Jesus commissions the disciples	Jesus appears in several places, then ascends to heaven	Jesus appears that day and the following week to the disciples

A few things worth noticing:

■ Mary Magdalene appears in all the accounts as the first to go to the tomb

■ There is no agreement about who greets them, and only one (Matthew) has an angel

■ Similarly, there is no agreement over who first encounters the risen Christ, or what happens after

Mary Magdalene: Apostle, not Prostitute

Mary Magdalene is among the first witnesses to the resurrection in all four gospels. She is the first person commissioned (by the risen Christ) to go out and tell the world that Christ is risen. And she has been brutally maligned by the church.

Such is the (brief) story of Mary Magdalene.

How did someone so vital to the resurrection stories in the gospels get to be seen as little more than a proverbial "woman of the night"? Probably the simplest answer is the correct one: she was a woman.

The gospels do not tell us much about Mary. We know that she was probably wealthy, being one of the women who supported Jesus' ministry. A wealthy woman was often seen as a threat to men, and so perhaps rumours begin to rise about how she acquired her wealth. We do not know, of course, but she may well have inherited it from her father or from a husband who was by that time deceased. The fact that she is known only by a regional moniker – Magdalene – rather than a man's name (daughter, wife, or mother of so-and-so) suggests that she is not "connected" to a man. This makes her both vulnerable in society, and susceptible to the teachings of Jesus, which emphatically tell her that she does *not* need to be attached to a man in order to have value.

We also learn that she has been exorcised of seven "demons" (Luke 8:2). Our mind may want to leap to images of the kind of beings associated with Halloween being driven from her body. But the Greek word used here, *daimonia*, can refer to almost any kind of ailment, including bacteria and viruses. Thus, a "demon" can be understood as an evil spirit (e.g., mental illness) or could simply be a common cold. It's possible to take the number seven literally, but because it was also traditionally used symbolically as the number of completion, it quite possibly could mean that she was "very" possessed; or it could be little more than a way of saying "she was really, really sick."

She becomes a disciple, which simply means that she followed Jesus. There is an intimacy alluded to, but this in no way implies sexual intimacy. If she was in fact not attached to a man, she might well have been ostracized from society, and so being accepted by Jesus and his community must have been a great relief.

In his biography of Mary Magdalene, scholar Bruce Chilton suggests that "Mary's gender presented no obstacle to her growing influence among Jesus' disciples. In fact, being a woman was consonant with her emerging power and authority as an expert on exorcism."

Yet Mary's rise quite probably led to her downfall. A woman of strength and power can leave men feeling weak and powerless. Early Christian writings, such as a third-century volume known as the *Didascalia of the Twelve Apostles*, reminds the church that they must revere deaconesses, because Jesus was himself ministered to by a number of deaconesses, including Mary Magdalene. This probably did not sit well with the early church. We also know that the Gospel of Thomas contains a rather stinging rebuke of Mary, with Peter saying in verse 114, "Let Mary depart from us, for women are not worthy of the life" – meaning the spiritual life of the resurrection community.

The gnostic *Gospel of Mary*, another ancient text, speaks of the male disciples being jealous because Mary "kisses" Jesus on the lips. Yet we barely need to scratch below the surface to discover an intriguing problem: the word translated as "kiss" is the Greek verb *aspazomai*; whenever it is used to reference men, it is translated as "greet," but with women it is translated "kiss." The problem here is not the ancient text, but our modern interpretation of it.

If all this were not enough, in 594 Pope Gregory the Great preached a sermon in which he openly declared Mary Magdalene a prostitute, even though there is absolutely nothing in any writing previous that even suggests it. (In a July 10, 2019, article in the *National Catholic Reporter,* Bill Tammeus says, "Think of it as sixth-century #FakeNews.") Gregory, in his mistaken wisdom, equated Mary with the woman who anointed Jesus' feet, who was commonly understood to be a prostitute (even though the Bible does not describe her that way), and by association paints Mary as a "cheap and wanton" woman. Whether Gregory meant this intentionally or not is subject to interpretation, but it had the effect of forever tarnishing Mary in the eyes of millions. Art since that time has served only to perpetuate the perception, with Mary often portrayed either scantily clad or naked, and often with a longing look in her eyes, as if craving a man. The rock opera *Jesus Christ Superstar* did not help, with its portrayal of Mary as a woman who sings that she has "had so many men before" and yet is in love with Jesus.

It was only in 1969 that the Roman Catholic Church officially declared that Mary was *not* a prostitute; clearly, old habits die slowly.

The larger debate needs to occur. Why has the Christian church so maligned – or, by saying nothing, permitted to be maligned – a person as biblically significant as Mary Magdalene? Why have we been so afraid to talk about and lift up the importance of a woman being sent out by the risen Christ to proclaim the good news? If Jesus had in fact begun a new community, where all those who had been marginalized were included, then does it not stand to reason that someone formerly marginalized should be brought front and centre? We must continue to ask such questions, and be bold with our answers. We must not let Mary Magdalene remain hidden in shadows.

Mary Magdalene's Legacy

The story of Mary Magdalene's encounter with the risen Christ near the tomb that first Easter morning is a profound reminder of what resurrection is really about, of that moment when the risen Christ calls us by name and we realize that, no matter what, we are included.

Mary Magdalene's Legacy

You have called me a whore
from the very beginning,
for two thousand years now
and Eve before me:
called us all whores
and witches
and worse.

You never bothered
to get to know me,
never wanted to ask me
    why are you alone?
    what is your story?
    who are you, really?
    how are you feeling?

The other disciples
from the twelve
through countless thousands
have discredited me
discredited us
called me a liar
a trouble-maker

a disruption
a nuisance
and worse.

I frustrate you.
I confound you.
For two thousand years
you have quietly
(and not so quietly)
wished I would go away.

When the others turned and fled
the cross,
and the tomb,
did you think I would flee, too?
Did you think I would give up?
How could I?
My life was too entangled with his.
(Oh no, I won't satisfy your cheap curiosity
with titillating gossip
and spill the beans here.)
No details
except to say that
had you not been so afraid of the stories of others
you might have learned a little more not only about me
but other disciples who ministered alongside Jesus,
learned of the work of so many more:
the women, the children, the also-rans.

But all that aside,
I never could have fled.
Despite all I endured
for three days,
for two thousand years,
I had to stay.

And in the silence,
in the waiting,
Christ came.

Louder than all of the scorn
    and the ridicule
    and the fear
    and the hatred,
louder than all of the lies
    and the misunderstandings
    and the abuse
    and the mistrust

Christ spoke my name:

    "Mary."

And I experienced resurrection.

It is that same Christ who commissioned me
to go and tell.

So I am here –
I have not gone away,
I will not go away.
As long as anyone, anywhere, is
    rejected
    cast aside
    spat upon
by the world – or,
worse still,
    by the church –
I am here
to proclaim the same truth
once told to me:

Christ Jesus is risen for you,
and calls you by name.
Let no one
    no one
ever tell you otherwise.

APPENDIX 3

Myth, Truth, and Fact

The Easter stories that tell us about encounters with the risen Christ are myth in the best, richest, and fullest sense of the word. A problem arises, however, when we use that word. It can make some people of faith very nervous because of the mistaken notion that the word myth means artificial or not true. However, that is not inherently the case.

The *Merriam-Webster* dictionary website offers this as a primary meaning of the word *myth:* "a usually traditional story of ostensibly historical events that serves to unfold part of the world view of a people or explain a practice, belief, or natural phenomenon." To put that another way, a myth is a story that may or may not be factual (more about that below) but that unfolds certain truths about a significant person, or helps to explain certain things. That tends to describe the stories about Jesus pretty well.

A further bit of definition from *Merriam-Webster* also says that a myth is "a popular belief or tradition that has grown up around something or someone." This is significant. The stories of Jesus are not well-corroborated outside of the Christian tradition, which can lead one to wonder about their historical accuracy. For many people of faith, especially in more conservative traditions, it seems vital to believe all the details about every story in the Bible, as if somehow the whole of faith might come crashing down if we were to introduce the element of doubt, even concerning tiny details. However, for many others, a broader, more open view can be not only helpful, but in fact freeing, and can contribute greatly to their

own faith journey. As Finnish scholar Lauri Honko put it, "A myth expresses and confirms society's religious values and norms."

While certain stories are quite believable and appear in almost identical form in more than one gospel, there are also times when they differ – to the point that both cannot be factual. At other times, stories include elements that stretch the imagination a little too far. Did Jesus, for example, somehow make a few bread rolls and some fish multiply miraculously before people's eyes? Did he really walk on water? And what about all those healings, which take place in a variety of different ways?

To understand the stories as myth can be very liberating, because it takes away the need to believe everything literally, and provides instead the opportunity to ask and explore how the stories can inform our lives. Let me give an example.

Many parts of the Bible challenge our logical minds. Other parts simply seem to contradict each other. We can try to pinch and squeeze and pretend certain details are not really there in order to take all these things literally, or we can take them metaphorically, which I believe

Mark 4:35–41

³⁵Later that day, when evening came, Jesus said to them, "Let's cross over to the other side of the lake." ³⁶They left the crowd and took him in the boat just as he was. Other boats followed along.

³⁷Gale-force winds arose, and waves crashed against the boat so that the boat was swamped. ³⁸But Jesus was in the rear of the boat, sleeping on a pillow. They woke him up and said, "Teacher, don't you care that we're drowning?"

³⁹He got up and gave orders to the wind, and he said to the lake, "Silence! Be still!" The wind settled down and there was a great calm. ⁴⁰Jesus asked them, "Why are you frightened? Don't you have faith yet?"

⁴¹Overcome with awe, they said to each other, "Who then is this? Even the wind and the sea obey him!"

makes them far stronger and more meaningful.

Read Mark 4:35–41 (see box). If we take this story literally, it has some intriguing benefit. For example, it tells us that should we happen to be in a boat on a lake, and Jesus is in the boat with us, and a storm comes up, Jesus can stop the storm and the boat will not capsize. That's good news, but it's very limited.

On the other hand, if we take the story metaphorically, it tells us that when life becomes extremely difficult – as if we're in the midst of a storm, as if there is no hope and we're sinking – if we realize that Jesus is with us, we can probably get through it. For me, that's carries a much stronger meaning and it has far more value for my day-to-day life. In other words, if we take the story metaphorically, it can apply to a far wider range of situations than if we take it literally, and it can have a stronger meaning for us. Such can be the power and value of myth.

Closely related to this is the tension between truth and fact. Many people readily equate the two, using them interchangeably. They understand a "true story" to be completely factual, yet such is not always the case.

Facts are things that can be proven (or disproven) and are, by nature, true. However, there are some truths that cannot be proven, yet they are still true. Here is an example from the Second World War.

Christian X was king of Denmark from 1912 through 1947. When Denmark was taken over by the Nazis, Christian refused to leave the country, and his defiance of the Nazis became legendary. It was well known that he would ride his horse through the streets of Copenhagen, unaccompanied by any guards, and this was a profound symbol for the Danish people of their ability to stand tall against the oppressor.

One day, a Danish boy was asked by a German soldier why the king rode without any guards, and the boy replied, "All of Denmark is his bodyguard." Another time, the Nazis attempted to fly the Nazi flag over the building being used as German army headquarters. The king told a German sentry that the flag must be removed. The sentry refused. The king then said, "I will send a soldier to take it down," and the sentry responded that the soldier would be shot. The king then declared, "That soldier will be me," and the flag was taken down.

The last – and probably most commonly repeated – story about King Christian concerns his decision, even though he wasn't Jewish, to wear a yellow star to show his solidarity with Danish Jews, who were required to wear a yellow Star of David. This in turn led many Danes to wear a yellow star, and this stymied Nazis plans to differentiate the Jews and imprison them.

These are wonderful stories. They tell us much about King Christian and about the history of the Danish people. They are arguably all true stories, for there is a kernel of fact in each of them. They tell us about the Dane's defiance of the Nazis, and about their support for the Jewish people. Facts, however, are harder to find here.

For example, it is a well-known fact (in Denmark at least) that the king rode his horse, undefended, around Copenhagen, which greatly bolstered the Danish people in their defiance of the Nazis. The Nazi flag only flew for one day over German army headquarters so there is good reason to guess that *something* happened, but no one really knows what.

It is also well known that the king helped many Jews escape from Denmark. However, Danish Jews were never compelled to wear the yellow star, and no Dane ever wore one, let alone the king.

These stories are not "factual"; they were clearly invented. Yet one could readily argue that they are true stories, for the truth they carry is strongly embedded in them: the king *did* defy the Nazis, and this in turn inspired many Danes to follow suit. The king *did* help many Jews escape to neutral Sweden, and this ostensibly inspired many Danes to do the same, thus preventing almost all of Denmark's Jews from being captured and imprisoned and/or killed.

Truth and fact do *not* need to be the same thing. There is a statue of Abraham Lincoln located in Park Square in Boston. It shows Lincoln standing over an African slave, pardoning him. Did Lincoln actually do this? Technically no. Yet he *did* do it on a much larger scale through his Emanicpation Proclamation. Such are truth and fact. Such is the case with much of the Bible.

BIBLIOGRAPHY

Brown, Raymond E. *The Gospel According to John.* Garden City, NY: Doubleday, 1970.

Chilton, Bruce. *Mary Magdalene.* New York: Doubleday, 2005.

— . *Rabbi Jesus: An Intimate Biography.* New York: Doubleday, 2000.

Craddock, Fred B. *Luke: A Bible Commentary for Teaching and Preaching.* Lousville, KY: Westminster John Knox Press, 1990.

Hare, Douglas R. A. *Mark.* Louisville, KY: Westminster John Knox Press, 1996.

— . *Matthew: a Bible Commentary for Teaching and Preaching.* Louisville, KY: Westminster John Knox Press, 2009.

Long, Thomas G. *Matthew.* Louisville, KY: Westminster John Knox Press, 1997.

Metzger, Bruce M. *A Textual Commentary on the Greek New Testament.* New York: United Bible Societies, 1975.

O'Day, Gail R. and Susan E. Hylen. *John.* Louisville, KY: Westminster John Knox Press, 2006.

Sloyan, Gerard. *John: a Bible Commentary for Teaching and Preaching.* Louisville, KY: Westminster John Knox Press, 2009.

Tammeus, Bill. "Author unravels the tangled identity of Mary Magdalene." *National Catholic Reporter,* July 10, 2019.

Williamson Jr., Lamar. *Mark: a Bible Commentary for Teaching and Preaching.* Louisville, KY: Westminster John Knox, 2009.

Death of Jesus
for Progressive Christians

A FIVE SESSION STUDY GUIDE

Donald Schmidt

While exploring the biblical stories about the death of Jesus, it is good to ask the larger question hanging in the background of all this drama: Why did Jesus die?

Contrary to atonement theory, scripture provides stronger responses to the question of why Jesus died. His message was revolutionary and a threat to the religious and political powers of the day. Talk of loving one's neighbours, of treating people as if they matter, of seeking forgiveness and new ways of being accountable to one another – these values do not encourage faithfulness to empire. Jesus' message was directly counter to the values that the government promoted. For them, there was no question but that Jesus had to be extinguished.

Similarly, the religious powers found their established order threatened. Jesus' theme of God's involvement in the world on behalf of the marginalized (specifically, foreigners, women, tax collectors, children, etc.) was a major challenge to the religious order of the day. It had to be stopped.

ISBN 978-1-77343-279-3
5.5" x 8" | 96 pp | paperback | $14.95

Birth of Jesus
for Progressive Christians

A FIVE SESSION STUDY GUIDE

Donald Schmidt

What if the Christmas story is not really what we think it is? What if things happened differently than tradition has maintained over the centuries? What if the biblical account differs – sometimes quite substantially – from the story most of us know from the nativity plays we participated in as children, or that our own children or grandchildren participate in? And what if the truth the authors of those stories are pointing to is not that Jesus was born in a miraculous way, but something that goes much deeper?

To some extent, each of us fashions our own version of the "Christmas story." Over time, as our associations and identification with that story grow, it can feel very uncomfortable and even disrespectful to disrupt or question that story. And yet these reactions can be instructive, for they beg larger questions about what's really important: the biblical narratives; or the traditions that have gathered around them, layered them, and at times obscured them; or the meaning all of this may have for our lives today?

ISBN 978-1-77343-287-8
5.5" x 8" | 80 pp | paperback | $14.95

Revelation
for Progressive Christians

A SEVEN SESSION STUDY GUIDE

Donald Schmidt

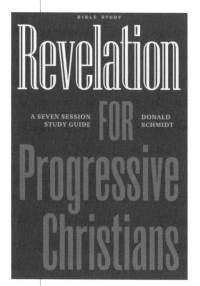

More material has probably been written about the biblical book of Revelation than the rest of the Bible combined – or at least it can seem that way. What's more, people who write or talk about Revelation often have a passion that defies all logic. They speak vividly and forcefully about plagues, and judgements, and the end of the world. All interesting themes – but are they the real concern or message of Revelation?

Revelation for Progressive Christians is a seven-session study guide that invites readers to explore Revelation as a fun, hope-filled book that contains a lot of fanciful imagery and symbolic references, to be sure, but that, at its core, offers words of assurance and hope to the church and its people today.

ISBN 978-1-77343-150-5
5.5" x 8" | 100 pp | paperback | $14.95

Passion & Peace
The Poetry of Uplift
for All Occasions

Compiled by Diane Tucker

All cultures we know of, at all times, have had poetry of one sort or another – chants, songs, lullabies, epics, blessings, farewells – to mark life's most important moments, transitions, and transformations. Ever since our species began using words, we have arranged them to please, to experience the pleasures, the fun, of rhythm and rhyme, repetition and pattern. *Passion & Peace: The Poetry of Uplift for All Occasions* was compiled to speak directly to this deep human need, with 120 poems from almost as many classical and contemporary poets, and including a thematic index. A welcome addition to any library and the perfect gift for any occasion, *Passion & Peace* is a heartwarming, uplifting, and inspirational volume.

ISBN 978-1-77343-028-7
6" x 9" | 304 pp | paperback | $24.95

Radical Gifts
Living a Full Christian Life in Troubled Times

Gene W. Marshall

In this new and and updated edition of his 1984 classic *A Primer on Radical Christianity*, Gene Marshall continues his "effort to envision for the general reader the *radical gifts* of the Christian revelation for the tasks of realistic living in our contemporary settings."

Progressive Christians will be immediately drawn to Marshall's discussions of "Spirit" sickness and how to heal it, his reflections on the nature of God, the relevance of the life of Jesus for people today, and the importance of community and of ethical thinking, which are as fresh and challenging today as they were when he first wrote on these topics. This edition features two new appendices, which contain updates to his original chapters on "ethical thinking" and "the community of the committed."

ISBN 978-1-77343-147-5
5" x 8.5" | 264 pp | paperback | $19.95

CPR for the Soul
Reviving a Sense of the Sacred in Everyday Life

Tom Stella

"The fact that you are not dead is not sufficient proof that you are alive!" So begins Tom Stella's insightful, important, and inspiring exploration into the life, death, and rebirth of the soul. He shares the deep, eternal wisdom that knows that the lines separating the sacred and the secular, time and eternity, humanity and divinity, are false. Or, at the very least, blurred. God, by whatever name, is found in the midst of everyday life, work, and relationships. All people, all creation, and all of life is holy ground. This remarkable book offers a revival for the soul, a reminder that "we are one with something vast" – a "something" that "is not a thing or a person, but a spiritual source and force at the heart of life."

ISBN 978-1-77343-039-3
5" x 8.5" | 248 pp | paperback | $19.95

WOOD LAKE

Imagining, living, and telling the faith story.

WOOD LAKE IS THE FAITH STORY COMPANY.

It has told
- the story of the seasons of the earth, the people of God, and the place and purpose of faith in the world;
- the story of the faith journey, from birth to death;
- the story of Jesus and the churches that carry his message.

Wood Lake has been telling stories for more than 35 years. During that time, it has given form and substance to the words, songs, pictures, and ideas of hundreds of storytellers.

Those stories have taken a multitude of forms – parables, poems, drawings, prayers, epiphanies, songs, books, paintings, hymns, curricula – all driven by a common mission of serving those on the faith journey.

Wood Lake Publishing Inc.

485 Beaver Lake Road
Kelowna, BC, Canada V4V 1S5
250.766.2778

www.woodlake.com